Original title:
The Quiet Power of a Brooch

Copyright © 2025 Creative Arts Management OÜ
All rights reserved.

Author: Riley Donovan
ISBN HARDBACK: 978-1-80586-064-8
ISBN PAPERBACK: 978-1-80586-536-0

A Pin's Silent Authority

A tiny little pin with grace,
Holds secrets in its clasped embrace.
In boardrooms filled with loud debates,
It gives a wink, as silence waits.

It sparkles bright, it twirls just so,
While gossip flies, it steals the show.
From shirts to coats, it struts its flair,
With every move, it claims the air.

The Brooch's Gentle Embrace

Nestled on a velvet dress,
It whispers softly, "I'm the best!"
Around the neck, or on the lapel,
With just a touch, it casts a spell.

It giggles when the sunlight beams,
In colors bold, or soft like dreams.
It nudges folks to take a glance,
A charming wink, a playful dance.

Radiance Worn in Silence

A glint of gold, a splash of red,
It holds the room without a tread.
Adorning jackets, blouses, ties,
With every glance, a small surprise.

With quiet class, it steals the scene,
No need for loud, it's rather keen.
It lifts the mood, it breaks the ice,
This tiny gem, it's oh so nice!

Subtle Strength of Pin and Stone

On fabric's edge, it finds its home,
A subtle strength, no need to roam.
It holds together what may flop,
A little hero, on the top.

With every twist, it finds its place,
In chaos swirls, it holds a space.
From fancy clubs to casual cafes,
This little pin brightens dull days.

Whispers of Gemstone Shine

On a coat, it sits so proud,
A tiny gem, a spark, a crowd.
With colors bold, it winks and scoffs,
As styles shift, it laughs and puffs.

Tiny heavyweight of flair,
It's magic, yes; no need to care.
The world may spin in chaos round,
But here's a jewel that must astound!

Glimmers of a Timeless Hold

In buttoned jacket, or evening gown,
It adds the flare to wearers' frown.
A glimmer here, a shimmer there,
It's only small, but hey, beware!

For with a flick and subtle twist,
It draws the eye; who could resist?
With pokes and prods, it steals the show,
Transforming attire with every glow.

The Stilled Conversation of Style

Oh, did you see that cheeky pin?
It's gossiping in whispers thin.
A nudge to say, 'I've seen it all,'
While capturing glances that make us fall.

In gatherings filled with chatter loud,
This fella speaks without a crowd.
A statement grand in so small a way,
Leaving us laughing at what it may say!

A Brooch's Kindred Spirit

My trusty pin, my fashion friend,
Through thick and thin, you always blend.
With every poke, you seal our pact,
Of stylish fun and wise impact.

In many shades, your quirks outshine,
A band that can make dull wear divine.
So here's to you, my shining mate,
With each little twist, we celebrate!

Metal and Memory Intertwined

On grandma's dress, it winks and beams,
A metal tale of long-lost dreams.
Each glint and sparkle, a secret dance,
Who knew it held such a funny chance?

It pinches me when I wear it right,
A rogue magician in plain sight.
It whispers jokes from times gone by,
And makes me chuckle as I walk by.

Enigma on Fabric

Nestled deep in silken seams,
A brooch that guards our silly dreams.
Its shape's a mystery, can't you see?
Is it a fish, or just a pea?

With each shimmering flash, a giggle peeks,
IT shines when life feels a bit bleak.
Hiding in plain sight, this shiny friend,
Keeps teasing twinkles that will not end.

Illuminated Shadows

In the corner, it plots and schemes,
Casting bright rays on dull regimes.
An outrageous character, never shy,
With a mischievous wink, it says hi!

A thimble, a heart, or maybe a shoe?
Its identity bends in colors anew.
It laughs in the light, prances in gloom,
A comedy star in the fabric room.

Reflections in a Single Pin

A simple pin, yet sets the stage,
For stories and laughter, ageless and sage.
It holds memories like a fish on land,
Just don't ask it to make a grand stand!

Each step I take, it jiggles and jives,
Reminding me of the silly lives.
With a glance in the mirror, a grin appears,
This small gem, my jokester for years!

Elegy in Adornment

In the drawer, tucked away tight,
A brooch waits for its grand night.
Once a star on a jacket's throne,
Now just a relic, all alone.

It dreams of gala, whispers of cheer,
But now it simply collects dust here.
Its glitter now dull, laughs like a fool,
Yet it swears, 'I was once super cool!'

The Legacy of Lapel

A little pin with grand ambitions,
Fancy embellishments, grand traditions.
Once a knight in a tuxedo's fight,
Now a sidekick, out of the light.

Oh, how it longs for a dance once again,
To stick to the flashy, and make 'em grin.
It dreams of tuxedos, bright ties, and flair,
Yet here it sits, like a lost millionaire.

Quiet Guardians of the Garment

Nestled in cloth, so sly, discreet,
A brooch guards secrets, doesn't admit defeat.
It keeps all the laughs from slipping away,
Once a fashion hero, now in dismay.

Who knew such an ornament hid such a sigh?
A custodian of deep fashion—oh my!
Yet every lapel it once kissed with grace
Now just admires its own empty space.

Softly Shimmering Truths

It sparkles soft, declares all is well,
A statement piece that's too proud to dwell.
Yet without a jacket, it just feels lost,
Just a shiny guardian, paying the cost.

A flicker of fun, a sprinkle of glee,
When worn, it's a party—just wait and see!
But left in a box, it can't help but pout,
'Who needs diamonds when I'm all about clout?'

A Pin's Legacy

A tiny pin on a woolly coat,
Brings laughter like a playful goat.
It's seen the world, worn proud and bright,
In the spotlight and even the night.

No one knows the tales it keeps,
Whispers of secrets, laughs, and leaps.
With just a clasp, it steals the scene,
A fashion force, so sly and keen.

Embers of Elegance

A little gem that sparks delight,
On every blouse, it shines so bright.
Its humor jiggles, makes us grin,
Like silly socks or playful kin.

Each evening out, it struts with flair,
Bright as a comet, light as air.
Who knew a checkered brooch could say,
"Look at my style, let's dance and play!"

Heartfelt Adornments

A brooch with heart-shaped, vibrant tones,
It laughs with joy, in fashion zones.
It holds our stories, one by one,
Like mismatched socks, it makes us fun!

With every twirl, it shows its might,
A wink of pastel in morning light.
It twinkles, it giggles, a little tease,
Wearing it brings us all to our knees!

Intimate Anchors

A tiny pin that anchors dreams,
Caught in the fabric, or so it seems.
It holds the stories of our days,
In bursts of color, laughter plays.

It guards our secrets, grand and small,
No one suspects, it's always on call.
With charm and cheek, it makes its mark,
A faithful friend, igniting the spark.

Significance Worn Close

A shiny little token, here I stand,
With stories in my clasp, oh so grand.
A pirate's secret stash, I'd love to keep,
But settled for a wardrobe, oh so deep.

My friends all gaze with puzzlement,
What's the point? They ask with sentiment.
But hidden in my sparkly dance,
Is mischief, daring, and a touch of chance.

When I pin myself to blazers crisp,
I sashay into rooms, feeling the lisp.
Dressed in finery, or just in jeans,
I bring the giggles, I've got the means.

Some call me silly, others a muse,
With every twinkle, I defuse the blues.
Like a classy little clown, I parade,
Spreading joy with every torque and fade.

The Emblem of Heartspace

I'm just a little gem on your lapel,
A tiny tale in sparkly shell.
You think I'm just for fashion and flair,
But I host secrets, treasures rare.

Broaches unite! We gather crowd,
Stitched together, oh so proud.
With stories only the brave can tell,
We're not just bling, we cast a spell.

Dear friends will giggle, as I gleam,
They'll poke and prod, and to me scream.
"What's your story? What's your job?"
I wink and nod, they all can blab.

I'm like a sock puppet, but all class,
Wearing me equals elegance, alas!
So next time you see me shine atop,
Remember, my charm will never stop!

Ornamented Secrets

In the corner, I glimmer with pride,
A humble spark that's hard to hide.
Little whispers of history worn thin,
Each clasp with a grin holds tales within.

I've witnessed first dates and kitchen spills,
Adventures unfurling on caffeine thrills.
Pinned on purpose and a tiny dare,
I may be small, but I'm loud as air!

Oh, the laughter shared, and jokes we've spun,
I'm the silent witness to all the fun.
On a winter coat or a summer dress,
My tiny glimmer brings out the best!

So poke fun, if you must, at my bling,
But watch the stories that I can bring.
I'm no ordinary metal with a gleam,
More like a comical dream team!

Poised in Silence

With just a flicker, I'm there in sight,
Holding together the daytime plight.
Fairy tales and puns, I keep them close,
An emblem of humor, a whimsical dose.

Friends might shake their heads and pout,
What's the fuss? They all shout out.
But pin me on, why don't you see?
I am the joy that sets you free.

I ride the wave of fashion's tide,
With silent laughter I do abide.
I'm a small dose of spark in a dreary room,
Bringing breezy laughs, dispelling gloom.

So when you spot me, don't look away,
I'm a giggle waiting to dismay.
Keep me close as the laughter flies,
In the world of fashion, I'm the surprise!

The Jewel's Gentle Power

A tiny sparkle on my chest,
It whispers secrets, oh so blessed.
It winks at those who take a glance,
A tiny gem, but what a dance!

With every day, it plays its role,
A feather weight, it scores its goal.
Makes a t-shirt feel like a dress,
Who knew a pin could cause such mess?

From work to play, it keeps me bright,
A chatty friend in plain sight.
While others flaunt their diamond crowns,
I just giggle, avoiding frowns.

So raise a cheer for bling that's small,
It knows to have a ball after all!

A Subtle Display

A dab of color on my lapel,
An icebreaker that casts a spell.
It's the cool kid at the party,
Quietly boasting, but so hearty!

When friends arrive, they always tease,
'What's your brooch, a flair of ease?'
With every poke and playful jab,
I smile while I give a fab!

It's not a grandiose affair,
Yet somehow, it gets all the stare.
Doodles, flowers, or something strange,
A small delight that knows no range.

I'm not a peacock, feathers bright,
Just a brooch, shining in twilight!

Stories Woven in Gold

Tales of yore made in gold,
Each curve and twist, a story told.
My little badge of past delight,
Spinning yarns both day and night.

From grandma's quilt to pirate's loot,
Every glance brings giggles, to boot!
In conversations, it sidelines,
While I laugh, the brooch unwinds.

'This one here? A fish from the sea!'
I say while it grins at you and me.
'And this one? A cupcake I'd never eat!'
A feast of memories, oh so sweet!

So on I go, fabric of dreams,
With a whispering brooch, laughter beams!

Unassuming Emblems

In crowded rooms, it sits, unseen,
A quiet jest, a little mean.
But come too close, and you'll take note,
It's a wizard in a fashion coat!

Whisked away to a fancy night,
I strut my stuff, feeling just right.
Compliments roll, 'Is that a pet?'
'No, it's my brooch, don't you forget!'

An ally in laughter where'er I roam,
It feels like I'm bringing my funny home.
Aside from that sparkly glare,
It's a friend who's always there to share.

So here's to the gems that steal our hearts,
In unassuming ways, they play their parts!

Grace and Solidity Intertwined

In a world where fashion sways,
A tiny gem holds the days.
It's pinned on coats and hats with flair,
A secret power's hiding there.

With silly shapes and colors bright,
It steals the show, a silly sight.
A matchstick brooch can raise a laugh,
Who knew a pin could steal the path?

Worn with a wink, or a playful pout,
This little piece can shout out loud.
A turtle charm on a fancy dress,
Transforming drab to fabulous mess!

So when you doubt your outfit's zest,
Just find a brooch, let fun manifest.
With quirk and charm, it takes the lead,
A tiny friend in fashion's steed.

The Allure of Weightlessness

A delicate pin, oh what a thrill,
Adorning blouses with a quirky chill.
A butterfly flutters, light as air,
Who knew a brooch could have such flair?

A tiny weight that holds such cheer,
Makes surfaces smile, seem more sincere.
On a pocket, it makes a mark,
Gathers giggles, ignites the spark!

It dances lightly with every move,
Gives no care, just wants to groove.
A moose on a jacket? Quite absurd!
Making heads turn, with hardly a word!

So let's rejoice in tiny things,
For lightness sometimes truly sings.
With silly flair, and laughter bright,
A little pin can spread delight!

Brooches as Bearers of Legacy

Once owned by grandma, now mine to wear,
An heirloom pin with quirky flair.
A cow on a chain that jigs a bit,
Tales of the past, where laughter lit.

With memories attached like the clasp so tight,
Each pin whispers secrets, oh what a sight!
A story shared, a chuckle wide,
In every piece of this family pride.

From feathery finds to strange designs,
These little wonders always entwine.
The milkman's brooch or a cat so sly,
Each carries legends, giving a sly eye.

So let's wear laughter sewn in our hearts,
Legacy shines in these playful parts.
Every pin a memento, a laugh, a cheer,
A shiny reminder of love held dear!

Shimmering Signals of Affection

A wink from a brooch, a glimmering kiss,
To share your love, it's hard to miss.
A heart-shaped gem, or a silly face,
Declarations of love, its playful grace.

It sits on your lapel, a flirty tease,
Says 'Hey there friend, come take it with ease!'
Each twinkling light a giggling trace,
Of friendships blooming in every space.

A pin shaped like pizza? It simply winks,
Unleashing laughter and playful links.
With humor and charm, it breaks the ice,
These tiny tokens can be so nice!

So wear your heart pinned to your coat,
Share giggles and joy, let laughter float.
For in each cute brooch, affection glows,
With shimmering signals of love that shows!

Unveiled Charisma

A little pin, a shiny flair,
It sits aloof, without a care.
In gatherings loud, it takes the stage,
With silent words, it starts to engage.

A modest gem, yet steals the show,
The crowd leans in, just for the glow.
What stories hide in tiny charms?
A wink, a grin, it spreads its arms.

Dancing round the collar's clasp,
It holds the party with a grasp.
While others boast with noise galore,
This little gem just wants to soar.

So let it sit upon your coat,
A gentle jest, a happy note.
In every glance, it gives a cheer,
And whispers jokes only you can hear.

Hidden Treasures of Elegance

A lonesome spark on fabric's face,
Whispering secrets with such grace.
In the corner, it twinkles bright,
Gossip mixed with pure delight.

An heirloom's charm, with tales to tell,
Of family feuds and laughs as well.
"Oh, that old thing?" they gasp with glee,
"It's more than meets the eye, you see!"

Adorning pockets, sleeves, and hats,
Like silent ninjas, they tease like cats.
With every tilt, a wink is thrown,
"Wear me proud, you're not alone!"

In this collection of winks and wiles,
Even the dullest scarf now smiles.
So let them shine, let them tease,
These tiny wonders aim to please.

The Strength of Stillness

A brooch that knows, without a sound,
How to keep the giggles wound.
It doesn't shout or make a scene,
Yet carries weight, light as a dream.

Worn with care, or tossed askew,
It holds its ground, while others flew.
In quirky shapes and colors bright,
It stands strong, a beacon of light.

The laughter swirls but it stays still,
A poised delight with subtle thrill.
It's not a cape, no flashy show,
But oh, the strength that it can show!

Each glance it catches, each giggle it lends,
In every heart, the joy transcends.
So wear it proud, let stillness reign,
A gentle power that feels like gain.

Brooches of Bated Breath

A brooch or two, they hold their breath,
Waiting for laughter, defying death.
In pauses long, they steal the air.
With ticklish charms, they sneak and dare.

Sitting sharp on blouses bright,
Stealing glances, igniting light.
What secrets come with every glare?
A hint, a jest, beyond compare.

In muted tones or colors loud,
They make you giggle, oh so proud.
A flick of light, a brush of sass,
In every twist, they're sure to amass.

So pin them down and watch them sway,
A twinkle here will save the day.
With laughter locked, just wait and see,
These tiny pins, a jubilee!

Threads of Elegance

On a coat, a jewel resides,
A twinkle that nobody hides.
With a wink, it steals the scene,
Like a magician, a fashion queen.

It whispers tales of style and flair,
In every gathering, it's always there.
One little pin and hearts will sway,
It's the sassiest of display.

When folks ask, 'Is that a cat?'
I reply, 'Nah, just a stylish hat!'
Girlfriends giggle, head's held high,
This tiny treasure never says bye.

It dances bravely on my chest,
My little secret, well-dressed guest.
In laughter's glow, it shines so bright,
A tiny crown in plain sight.

The Gentle Hold of History

Once pinned on a queen, or so they say,
Now it rests on me, hip-hip-hooray!
A relic of laughter, time's posh muse,
From past to present, it's got the moves.

It holds the weight of silly glee,
When paired with jokes over afternoon tea.
Histories clash, humor prevails,
With a brooch that never fails!

As dinner's served, it takes a bow,
'Look at me! I'm still in style now!'
Chitchat echoes, everyone sees,
This brooch can make the dullest tease.

With every sparkle, there's a wink,
It laughs at time, watches us think.
Forever may it hang in joy,
Making every moment coy.

A Pinch of Grace

Just a little pin, a sprinkle of fun,
A fashion statement, second to none.
With colors bold and stories bright,
It catches glances, day or night.

In quirky shapes that tell a tale,
Worn upside down, it'll never fail.
A pinch of grace with a wink in tow,
Shining bright, putting on a show!

At parties, it steals a laugh or two,
Who knew such flair could come from glue?
With one little twist, it spins around,
Transforming outfits, lighter than sound.

Lipstick smudged and hair a mess,
Still, this brooch demands no less.
It struts unapologetically,
Spreading mirth like a jubilee.

Stories Worn Close

Every pin has its quirky flair,
From a peaceful dove to a wild bear.
It brings to life the tales we share,
Hidden mischief, love, and dare.

When I wear it, can't help but smile,
Reminiscing journeys, mile after mile.
Friends gather round, eyes aglow,
What stories lie beneath, who knows?

'Is that a vintage shark?' they cry,
'It's been on more trips than you or I!'
A bond of laughter, stitched in thread,
With every glance, a joke is bred.

It laughs with me through thick and thin,
Each brooch a trophy, laughter wins.
And as we dance, I gladly boast,
These memories? Oh, I wear the most!

An Echo of Elegance

A tiny pin with flair, so bright,
It sparkles subtlety in light.
On jackets worn or bags so fine,
It winks with charm, a bold design.

In meetings drab, it starts to glow,
Of secret tales that few will know.
"A brooch," they say, "is just a clasp,"
But oh, the style! It makes us gasp!

Like instant flair in a dull sea,
A jester dressed in finery.
With each small twist, it dances so,
And makes us laugh, 'Oh look at you go!'

A whimsy held against the skin,
With just one pin, the fun begins.
So wear it proud, let laughter stream,
Your little gem—a fashion dream!

Unfurling Grace

With laughter stitched in every seam,
They say it's just a little gleam.
Yet hidden tales tucked in its fold,
An antique story to be told.

This little spark is quite the tease,
It makes us smile with such great ease.
On grandma's coat, it found its home,
Through decades past, it loves to roam.

It flutters bright, a tiny bird,
In worlds of fashion—quite absurd!
"Is it a brooch?" you might just quip,
Or is it magic on an epic trip?

A secret pact with style and jest,
In this small pin, the world's a fest.
So wear it, flaunt it, don't forget—
This sparkly joy is full of wit!

The Alliance of Brooch and Heart

The little pin links heart and soul,
An ally perfect to make one whole.
It bridges moments, old and new,
With every glance, it smiles at you.

In fabric soft or leather tough,
It whispers, "Life's a playful stuff!"
"We're in this together!" it seems to say,
With a wink and twist, it leads the way.

In curious places, it likes to peek,
From pockets deep to cuffs unique.
"Who wore that?" they giggle and cheer,
As the tiny brooch proves it's got no fear.

So gather 'round for a fashion chat,
With flair and humor, let's have a spat.
In each small twist of shiny art,
A cute reminder of joy at heart!

Silent Theater of Style

In a world where boldness struts about,
This little brooch flickers, no doubt.
No need for thunder or great display,
It's simply chic in a quiet way.

With velvet hues and some glitter too,
It brings the laughs, it's simply true.
"What's that?" they ask, "A tiny star?"
"It's just your style, shining from afar!"

So let it dance on your Lapel fine,
In its soft grace, a hint of wine.
No Broadway song or grand ballet,
Just chuckles shared throughout the day.

An understated joy, a petal's sway,
In its small world, we laugh and play.
So wear your pin, in your own view—
It's the best-kept secret between me and you!

A Pin's Serene Majesty

Upon my chest this shiny plan,
A tiny pin, a mighty fan.
It glistens bright, a tiny star,
Commanding grace, both near and far.

In meetings drab, it gives a wink,
While ties and suits are on the brink.
It tells a tale of fun and flair,
With just a pin, I rock the air.

It holds together thoughts and dreams,
While laughter bubbles, light it seems.
With every glance, it steals the show,
My subtle charm, my badge of glow.

So here I sit, chic and sly,
With mighty threads that wave and fly.
A pin again, it wins the day,
In silly games, I find my way.

Sentiments Cast in Metal

A mystery pinned upon my dress,
With tales untold, I must confess.
It jingles softly, a quirky tune,
Like early birds or late afternoon.

This little token, held so tight,
Is sass and humor, pure delight.
With every poke, I share a jest,
A metal friend—my fashion quest.

It speaks of love, of silly things,
Adventures wrapped in cherished rings.
With each new friend that comes my way,
My shiny story finds its play.

So here I stand, proud and bright,
With humor dressed in gleaming light.
A laughing piece that can't be lost,
It brings me joy, whatever the cost.

The Softness of Strength

A brooch of bloom rests near my heart,
Whispers humor, a playful art.
It hides a quirk, a gentle boast,
A metal smile, my trusty host.

Among the serious, it dares to shine,
A spark of joy along the line.
In meetings tense, it steals the day,
A giggle here, a laugh at play.

Oh, how it glimmers, joyous zest,
A soft reminder; life is best.
With every twist and little turn,
My charming gem, I live and learn.

So let it dance and let it twirl,
Through serious times, it makes me whirl.
A statement piece of fun and cheer,
In every glance, it draws them near.

Brooch of Belonging

A tiny thing, yet fits just right,
In colors bold, a welcome sight.
It holds my stories, laughs, and dreams,
A cozy spark in life's grand schemes.

This charming piece has friends galore,
Each one adds flavor, helps restore.
Through silly chats and laughter loud,
My little brooch, it stands so proud.

With every clasp, it says, 'You're mine,'
A bond that laughs, a thread divine.
In gatherings strange, it feels like home,
A badge of joy wher'er I roam.

So here's to pins that make us grin,
A symbol that reminds within,
That joy in metal, bright and strong,
Is where we laugh and all belong.

Pinning Down Truths

A little pin, oh what a sight,
It holds my hopes, it holds my plight.
With every clasp, a story's told,
In metal shimmers, truth unfolds.

It's not just flair, it's a sly wink,
Each color tells what I don't think.
I wear it high, I wear it low,
A fashion statement, or just for show?

With glitter bright, and sass so bold,
It whispers secrets, never old.
You think it's small? Well, think again,
This little gem has got a pen!

So here's the truth, let's share a laugh,
A tiny pin can steal the path.
From pocket fluff to royal glee,
A brooch's worth is more than free!

The Elegance of Restraint

A tiny dot of glint and shine,
It sits so sweet, almost divine.
Not loud or wild, it gives a nod,
A wink of class, oh isn't that odd?

With each soft poke, a giggle sewn,
A flair so chic, yet all alone.
"It's just a brooch," one might say,
But in the crowd, it steals the play.

Simplicity! Fashion's subtle game,
A tiny piece that raises fame.
Worn with a grin, or just a grin,
This understated gem knows how to win.

So praise the pin, it knows its worth,
In lovely ways, it finds its birth.
The simplest things can make us beam,
Who knew a brooch could fuel a dream?

Preserved in Precious Metals

Metal glimmers, stories abound,
In tiny forms, old tales are found.
A lock of hair, a lover's touch,
In shiny trinkets, they matter much.

They'll never break, nor fade away,
As life drifts on, they choose to stay.
With every snag, a tale unfurled,
Each twist and turn, a tiny world.

In gilded hues and silver tones,
They guard our hearts, they guard our bones.
A laugh, a sigh, a wink, a cheer,
These little pins, they hold us dear.

So raise a glass to gems so bright,
With every pin, we catch the light.
In whimsy's grasp, their charm enchains,
A fabric woven with laughter's strains!

The Art of Subtlety

With gentle grace, a tiny piece,
It knows just when to bring some peace.
In crowds so loud, it takes a spot,
A tender touch weaving the knot.

You'll find it tucked, or on display,
In simple lines, it steals the day.
A cheeky twist, a wink of flair,
It's quiet fun, without a care.

A seasoned pro, this brooch, you see,
It knows the art of mystery.
In whispers soft, it shares a joke,
With every sparkle, laughter's cloak.

So here's to pins, both small and bright,
Their quiet charm, a pure delight.
They dance on threads, in playful spin,
With just a flick, they let us win!

The Elegance of Undercurrents

In a sea of chaos, she takes her stand,
A tiny spark, yet oh so grand.
With a wink and a nod, it whispers away,
Turning heads in the most subtle way.

A pinch of whimsy rests on her chest,
It knows how to charm, it knows how to jest.
A curious gaze asks, what's that you wear?
She laughs and replies, 'Just a little flair!'

While others flaunt gems, shining so bright,
She twinkles with mischief, a true delight.
In the banquet of life, she's the perfect tease,
A friendship forged with the smallest of keys.

So here's to the clasp that likes to play,
It dances in shadows, keeps dullness at bay.
With elegance hidden, in laughter it flows,
A secret companion, as only it knows.

An Enchantment in Stillness

A brooch of whimsy, a laugh in disguise,
Nestled on fabric, beneath watchful eyes.
It grins at the mundane, a wink at the sane,
Ready to spice up the run-of-the-mill plain.

Glimmering gently, it plots and it schemes,
In the stillness of life, it weaves all the dreams.
With a chuckle so soft, it plays through the day,
Changing the course in a most clever way.

When the crows gather round in their meeting of caw,
This little distraction gives them pause and awe.
For in all the chatter, a secret it bears,
A story of laughter tucked under the stairs.

Oh, the tales it could tell, if only it spoke,
Of moments lost in the mist of a joke.
But behind velvet petals, in stillness it sits,
A kingdom of joy where the laughter admits.

A Quiet Jewel's Journey

He set off on a journey, this jewel so sly,
With a heart full of giggles, he'll never say die.
Sliding through pockets and sneaking through seams,
Chasing the sunset, unfolding the dreams.

Each hitchhiked adventure, a tale yet untold,
With laughter to warm him, through snows bitter cold.
He tickled a scarf and teased a tall hat,
With a twirl and a whirl, just imagine that!

In cafés and concerts, he brightens the gloom,
Bringing a twist to a boring costume.
With every new twist, with every surprise,
He twinkles and chuckles, under whimsical skies.

As the lights softly dim, and the night starts to hum,
He glimmers like magic, 'Oh, how fun!'
So raise up a toast to the journeys out wide,
Of a quiet little gem with wild joy inside.

The Trace of Timelessness

In a box of treasures tucked away,
Lies a gem with tales to say.
It once danced boldly on a coat,
Now it's shy, but still, it wrote.

A pin that's seen both dusk and dawn,
Adventures from a world long gone.
It holds the laughter, sparks the cheer,
A tiny hero, held so dear.

With every glance, a giggle shared,
Of all the outfits it once paired.
Worn with a wink, or styled with flair,
It sparks delight beyond compare.

So here's to brooches, small yet grand,
With hidden stories that expand.
A simple clasp, yet full of glee,
A wink from fashion history.

Mementos of the Heart

A sparkly clip from years gone by,
It's got a look that makes you sigh.
It's a laugh from days when life was free,
A trinket's worth is hard to see.

It rides the lapel like a carefree bird,
In colors that are slightly absurd.
It whispers sweet nothings to the dress,
"Oh darling, you were one of the best!"

It's been to weddings and picnics, too,
When it peeks out, it bids adieu.
It spruces up a drab old threads,
With just one twinkle, it lightly treads.

So wear it proudly, let it shine,
This charming piece of yours, divine.
Keep it close, a memory so smart,
A memento, oh, the joy it can impart!

A Stitch of Strength

A little brooch of dainty size,
A stitch of strength, oh what a surprise!
Once an angel, now a bear,
Worn on a whim, with nary a care.

It holds together all the fray,
A knight in glitter, come what may.
With just a wink, it lifts the day,
It's more than metal, it's here to stay.

Imagine the tales it could recite,
From morning's calm to the wild night.
It's saved a hem, kept style intact,
A tiny force, that's a real fact!

A stitch, a clasp, a charming plea,
The strength in smallness, can't you see?
Wear it with pride, like your finest crown,
For strength can sparkle, never drown!

Radiance in Restraint

A twinkle here, a shimmer there,
This little brooch, beyond compare.
It grins from collars, quietly bold,
A secret smile, a story told.

In the world of jewels, it plays it cool,
Not flashy, just clever, it breaks the rule.
With gentle charm, it takes the lead,
An unassuming hero, indeed!

A wink of brass, a dash of grace,
Completes the look, without a trace.
Subtle brilliance, like a good pun,
Doesn't have to shout, it has the fun!

So let it twinkle in the sun,
A radiant laugh, a playful run.
In every clasp, resilience flows,
A little sparkle, that truly glows!

Threads of Quiet Intention

On a coat, it clings so tight,
Whispering tales of charm and might.
A twinkle here, a wink of thread,
Smiles are sewn where worries fled.

Underneath the laughter's flow,
Winks to secrets no one knows.
With just a pin, a twist, a turn,
Fashion's fire begins to burn.

Brooches dance in stories shared,
In corners where no one dared.
They wink and giggle, slight mischief,
As if to say, "I'm quite the chief!"

So raise a glass to shiny friends,
Whose silent sass rarely ends.
In the fold of every seam,
Lies a wink, a sparkling dream.

The Jewel's Veiled Authority

Nestled in a velvet nest,
A gem's quick glance—could it be best?
It juggles class while stirring cheer,
With just a dash of playful sneer.

A bit of sparkle, nothing grand,
Yet on you, it takes a stand.
Like an eye with secrets tight,
Sassy whispers take to flight.

Worn with humor, worn with style,
A subtle wink—a cheeky smile.
It struts about with quiet glee,
Pretending it's the royalty!

So here's to those, both bold and shy,
Brooches say, "Give life a try!"
With a clip or a twirl, they reign,
Keeping laughter in their chain.

Flashes of Forgotten Elegance

In the cabinet, dust does blend,
A bygone friend, a vintage trend.
It sparkles shyly, just a pinch,
With stories that make laughter cinch.

Once the toast of swanky balls,
Now it giggles from the walls.
"Look at me," it seems to say,
"Time can't dull my fierce ballet!"

Like a ninja in the night,
It flashes whimsy, what a sight!
Sipping tea, it holds court proud,
With punchlines only it allowed.

So dust it off, let laughter cling,
An heirloom that can make hearts sing.
Hidden gems, with tales to weave,
Whisper joy, and we believe.

Constellations in Precious Form

Pinned upon a cardigan neat,
It maps the cosmos with its beat.
Stars aligned in cheeky glee,
Datetime wonders—just for me!

It's a universe on my lapel,
A cosmic joke; oh, can't you tell?
Planets twirl and galaxies spark,
In the daylight or in the dark.

With every twinkle, dreams take flight,
Tales of whimsy, day and night.
A brooch that giggles with delight,
As if to say, "Go, hold me tight!"

So toast the stars with little flair,
With every pin, there's laughter shared.
In precious shapes, they come alive,
Little joys that always thrive.

Tales of the Unseen

In the corner sat a pin, quite sly,
It winked at the world, oh so spry.
A secret life under fabric's guise,
Holds tales of wonder, beneath the wise.

A glimmer here, a shimmer there,
It plots and plans without a care.
Fending off collars that threaten to droop,
With style supreme, it leads the troop.

An ally for scarves, and ties that may droop,
The silent negotiator, supreme in the loop.
Dressed in delight, with humor to spare,
It chuckles at rivals, unaware of its flair.

So laugh with your brooch, let it shine bright,
A quirky companion in day or in night.
For what's hidden beneath is a treasure untold,
A beacon of laughter, both young and old.

Symbolism in Silence

A little gem nestled, snug and tight,
Swaps gossip with fabric, oh what a sight.
No loud proclamations, no need to shout,
Just subtle suggestions that leave folks in doubt.

It tickles the pastel of a drab old coat,
With a wink of its shine steals focus from rote.
Behind every lapel, it keeps scores with flair,
In a world of the noisy, it breathes fresh air.

And should you address it, it blushes in glee,
"Did you see my dance? Just wait, let it be!"
In the halls and the parties, it hums a new tune,
While the echoes of laughter skip over the moon.

So don't ever doubt this silent delight,
As it giggles and glimmers, oh what a flight!
In whispers of fashion, it reigns supreme,
The quiet little rebel that rules every dream.

The Jewel's Quiet Declaration

Nestled snug on jackets quite grand,
This tiny jewel takes a firm stand.
No thunderous fanfare, but hints of cheer,
With a playful nod, it draws us near.

In museums of fashion, it takes the spotlight,
With tales of past glam, and style just right.
It teases and pleases with every glance,
Turning dull moments into a dance.

"A pin!" they exclaim, with eyebrows raised high,
Yet it knows that this trinket can soar and fly.
With every outfit, it sets off the spark,
Like a jester's jest in a world that's dark.

So strut with your bauble, let laughter ring clear,
For this little jewel is a dear charmer, my dear.
A quirky companion of whimsy and jest,
In the realm of the mundane, it stands out the best.

Graceful Authority

A brooch, so bold with its gentle style,
Can declare you the boss, while flashing a smile.
It knows how to lead, without making a fuss,
While all else around just fall into bus.

When pinning down meetings with trivial talk,
It beams from the lapel like a peacock's walk.
With a wink and a nod, it commands the stage,
The true CEO under the fashion page.

Promoting good times with a wink and a grin,
It holds court in silence, yet welcomes you in.
With threads and with patterns, it starts the spree,
Oh, the joy in the room, where it rules undividedly.

So here's to the brooch, a sage of delight,
A master of charm, with infinite might.
In the world of attire, where chaos may rise,
It brings us together and cuts through the lies.

Echoes of a Jewel's Sentiment

In the corner it sits, a silent spark,
It sparkles at feasts, but waits in the dark.
Chattering at parties, it steals the show,
Yet at home, it's simply a place for a bow.

With stories locked tight in its shiny embrace,
It giggles at wearers in a colorful race.
While the necklace brags loud about bling and fame,
This little gem whispers, "Hey, I'm not lame!"

When pinned to a jacket, it has some flair,
A dance of nostalgia fills up the air.
It nudges and pokes with a glint of jest,
Making even the grumpiest feel feeling blessed.

So let's toast to the gem, small but unbound,
A jokester at heart, it's wit knows no sound.
For in every clasp, and in every twist,
Lies a humor-filled story, too fun to resist.

Subdued Glamour

In a pocket it hides, a sassy delight,
While tassels swing wildly, it laughs at the sight.
With its pins and its bends, joys buried in gold,
Whisper secrets of shimmer, stories untold.

It sits on a blouse like a queen on her throne,
Drawing eyes, yet it grins, "I'm cool on my own!"
As glittering giants strut past with a frown,
This simple adornment wears a soft crown.

Jewelry can shout, but this one contains,
A ticklish reminder that wit still remains.
Strutting through life with a calm little nod,
It silently mocks the flashy facade.

So here's to the charm, both timid and bold,
With humor tucked in every fold.
A knotted smile on a fabric ground,
In its understated glory, true joy can be found.

Unseen Yet Unyielding

Hiding in shadows, full of surprise,
A playful glint dances, teasing the eyes.
It's there on the lapel, quite modest and sly,
Stealing the spotlight as it winks by and by.

While others all flaunt with their jewels on display,
This treasure quietly chuckles, keeping cringe at bay.
"I'm here for the laughter, not just for the bling,"
A stubborn little icon, a feather in its wing.

Daring the world to take it for granted,
It giggles each time when it feels so enchanted.
The shapeshifting gemstone knows how to blend,
Sassy yet humble, a truly great end.

So let's raise a toast, for the bold and the small,
The laughs we can share, the glee of it all.
In the dance of the delicate, a wink and a smile,
Our unseen companion makes life's joy worthwhile.

The Weight of a Whisper

Clasped to a coat, like a secretive friend,
Its murmurs of mischief seem never to end.
With a twinkle of charm, it invites to explore,
As laughter erupts, it whispers for more.

A gentle reminder, when days seem too thick,
A playful distraction, a delicate trick.
"Did you hear that? Just a laugh and a tease!"
It bolts from the pocket, making hearts freeze.

In the chatter of clinks, and the cheer of the crowd,
This hidden gem chuckles, soft yet so loud.
As others brag boldly of grandiose things,
This brooch brings delight, and joy that it brings.

So let's shine for the joy, the small but the grand,
In a world that's so noisy, it's laughter we stand.
For in every whisper, there's power so spry,
A quiet committee of joy flying high.

Whispers of Adornment

In the corner of a room, she sat,
A tiny spark of fancy chat.
A brooch, a wink, a playful breeze,
It laughed and danced with such great ease.

A flicker at a meeting's start,
With mischief scripted in its heart.
A hidden giggle, a tiny tease,
Such charm concealed with utmost ease.

As people squinted, 'What's that glint?',
Her brooch just winked, without a hint.
It took the stage with subtle grace,
A party-crasher at the place.

Dressed in sequin, gold, or jade,
It played with light, a masquerade.
Who knew a pin could hold such fun?
A meeting turned to jest — well done!

Embers Beneath the Stone

A little gem on lapel so bright,
Hiding secrets, oh what a sight!
It smirks at all who walk on by,
A tiny ember, 'I won't lie!'

At lunchtime, it spills a softer glow,
Telling tales of where it would go.
Each twinkle tells a playful lie,
An icebreaker with every sigh.

From boardroom gloom to café cheer,
This little charm can bring good cheer.
With bated breath, it takes a bow,
And silent laughs ensue, somehow.

Like spy in shadows, it sat so bold,
With stories of glitter and laughter told.
No need for whispers when it's this keen,
For in its shimmer, joy can be seen!

Unveiled Secrets in Silver

A polished pin of silver hue,
It holds the tales of me and you.
Each flicker whispers tales of days,
Intrigues wrapped in glittery ways.

A board-game piece on a shirt so plain,
It pokes fun at normal's reign.
A hero's cloak, it claims the spot,
While others miss what it has got.

In board meetings, it swirls and sways,
A slick remark, it always plays.
When idle hands fidget and roam,
That lively pin might call them home.

So here's the scoop—don't take it light,
A sparkly ally in every fight.
With its small charm and gentle jest,
A playful brooch is always best!

A Jewel's Silent Promise

Nestled on fabric, it takes its stand,
A pearl of wisdom, soft and grand.
It promises laughs although discreet,
With every smile, it skips a beat.

In a world where whispers rhyme,
It tells a joke, it wastes no time.
Dapper or casual, it sways just right,
A little sparkle to bring delight.

At parties, it's the silent bard,
With stories shared but never marred.
In laughter's wake, it glows and gleams,
This humble token knows our dreams.

So wear a trinket, relax, and share,
Unearth the fun hidden somewhere.
With every glance, it hints and smiles,
In subtle ways that stretch for miles.

The Keeper of Memories

In a drawer of forgotten dreams,
Lies a bauble that subtly gleams.
A relic of awkward teenage dances,
With big blue stones and silly chances.

It held my hair, kept secrets tight,
A guardian of my most vivid night.
Did it know I tripped on my own shoe?
I guess it had a laugh or two.

Each pin transformed with zealous might,
An ace at the games of awkward fright.
From prom to picnics, it wore it proud,
Unraveled chaos, a sparkling shroud.

Now on my coat, it winks and beams,
Sharing old tales in whispered themes.
With every button, it sends a shout,
Memories tucked in glittering rout.

Sparkle Underneath Solitude

Pinned upon the lapel quite keen,
A shimmered secret, a spark unseen.
It snickers softly in lonely hours,
Winks at boredom, sprouts wild flowers.

Tucked beneath layers, hides its glee,
Turning mundane into a jubilee.
With every glance, it starts a show,
A studded muse in its own glow.

Dull meetings perk up with a glint,
What's that? A story, a blurry hint.
While I nod seriously, it winks and sighs,
A jester in disguise, oh how time flies!

In solitude, it knows how to tease,
Painting my day with strokes of ease.
Just a brooch, but oh, what flair!
It giggles at drudgery, light as air.

Stories Stitched in Color

A circle with stories, spun so bright,
Worn on my collar, a funny sight.
It tells of adventures, of highs and lows,
As it stitches together my life's quick shows.

With yellows and blues in playful curls,
It hints at mischief when I twirl.
"Remember that time?" it whispers to me,
Of crazy antics and wild jubilee.

An old cat's eye, a dragonfly's wing,
Each charm a memory, each laugh a fling.
In family tales, it's the punchline, you see,
Transforming history into a comedy spree.

With every wear, it adds a jest,
Those little moments that feel the best.
Stories stitched in color, who would know?
Just me and my brooch stealing the show!

A Brooch's Timeless Whisper

A tiny whisper rests on my dress,
A jeweled talent in vintage finesse.
It nudges me gently, a charming guide,
Through outfits so bland, it takes me for a ride.

Worn at the breakfast, or evening's delight,
It sparkles ever so lightly at night.
With a nod and a swirl, within the crowd,
It giggles softly, yet stands so proud.

It knows my wardrobe more than I do,
An expert in sass with its quiet view.
"Try the polka dots!" it says with glee,
Who knew fashion was crafty as me?

As if in a sketch, it winks to the sheen,
Playing the role of the life unforeseen.
A brooch, what tales could it lend?
When style meets laughter, it's a trendy blend!

Shimmering Stories in Stillness

Upon my chest, a tiny spark,
A brooch that twinkles in the dark.
It whispers tales of times gone by,
And makes me laugh, oh my, oh my!

It's not just gold, but stories told,
Of grandmas young and legends bold.
With every glance, a chuckle flows,
A wink that only fashion knows.

A cheeky cat with emerald eyes,
It prances proudly, oh what a prize!
"When did cats start wearing gems?" I muse,
As folks around me, lightly snooze.

A quirky dance, a jolly flair,
A pin that says, "I just don't care!"
With every sway, it steals the show,
And leaves a trail of giggles aglow.

The Elegance of Detour

A lady's pout adorned with grace,
A single brooch, a witty face.
It points the way to snappy fun,
And winks at all, like it has won.

Oh dear, a squirrel in a hat,
Who knew such style could make them chat?
Just pinned on, it breaks the mold,
Where serious thoughts dare not unfold.

A disco ball on a soft pink dress,
It twirls away my morning stress.
With every tilt, a giggle spark,
Just watch it shine, a little lark!

"Where's your message, Mr. Pin?"
I ask myself, with a cheeky grin.
But in its shimmer, there's a tease,
A silent tale, a funny breeze.

A Fragment of Serenity

A humble pin upon my thread,
Steals the limelight, oh, how it spreads!
With pearl and gold, it winks at me,
"Wear me right, and you will see!"

It's a dragonfly doing ballet,
Dazzling all in its own way.
"Am I a bug or am I art?"
I can't help giggling, what a smart!

A pop of color in a dull day,
It hums a tune; who'd dare to sway?
Like a hummingbird on a quest,
It flutters near, and I feel blessed.

"Where do you go when I'm not near?"
It chuckles back, "I spread good cheer!"
A secret bond, just us, we play,
In quiet moments, come what may.

Gestures in Gem

A jester's hat upon my chest,
With colorful gems, it feels the best.
Each twinkle tells a joke or two,
An audience of laughs, who knew?

Earrings drop and fall away,
But on my garment, here to stay.
A little whimsy, cheeky grace,
With every turn, it finds its place.

A taco shaped in sparkling light,
"Eat me, but don't take a bite!"
It flares with joy, it brings good vibes,
As smiles spread and laughter jibes.

A timid fool wrapped in a pin,
It tells me stories thick and thin.
In every sparkle, every glint,
Lies a world where humor's hinted.

The Art of Subtlety

A brooch perched high, a sly little wink,
It holds more stories than we often think.
It sparkles with mischief, a twinkle in flight,
A conversation starter, as day turns to night.

With just a small pin, it claims its own space,
A dragonfly dancing, a smile on its face.
In meetings and dinners, it steers the whole show,
You think it's a brooch, but it's really a pro!

With colors that clash, yet somehow combine,
Fashion faux pas? No, it's quite divine.
It raises eyebrows, doubles the fun,
A chaotic companion, second to none.

So wear it, don't hide it, let it have glee,
This brooch has a life, as cheeky as he.
A gem of small charm, yet larger than life,
Its antics and whimsy cut through any strife.

Whispers of Adornment

Upon my lapel, a little bird sings,
It chirps tales of fashion, and other small things.
Its colors confuse all who glance at it quick,
Is it art? Is it nature? Just take your pick!

Behold my fine brooch, a leaf made of jade,
It might just be costumed; a leafy charade.
It scoffs at the rules of what style should be,
Craving attention, though trying to flee.

A comet, a squirrel, an odd-looking hat,
Each pin holds a secret, a giggle, a chat.
In the realm of the subtle, it's king of the jest,
When elegance fails, it just loves the mess.

Whispers roll out; they're meant to be heard,
This sly little poker is quite the small bird.
A flicker, a swap, unexpected delight,
The laughs it conceals make the evening just right.

Secrets in Silver

In silver so sly, a riddle's confined,
A brooch with a secret, but who's ever aligned?
A moth, a moonbeam, it wears like a crown,
This pinched little creature just laughs through the frown.

It winks at the crowd, but they don't quite see,
Its jewels have stories, whimsical glee.
When caught in a glance, it flutters about,
Delivering joy with an offhanded shout.

In front of the mirror, I chuckle and grin,
This glittery gem hides a giggle within.
With one tiny clip, I lift spirits in air,
From here to Manhattan, it'll whisk you with flair.

So hand me my silver, let's go for a spin,
In quiet capers, that's where we begin.
Endeavors in fashion, with laughs all around,
This secret of silver is charm unbound.

Elegance Encased in Gemstone

A ruby so bright, it steals all the light,
Encased in a gem, it dazzles by night.
With humor it sparkles, a cheeky delight,
A wink and a grin, it's a fashionable sprite.

This jewel upon velvet just loves to show off,
It's funny how some find humor in cloth.
When strangers do squint, it's hard not to laugh,
A delicate pinch – if only they asked!

Dancing with diamonds, it twirls on its stage,
A sassy little pin with a witty engage.
In crowded pool parties or tea with the queen,
It tosses a wink as if planning a scene.

Is it fancy, is it fun? A mystery known,
A brooch full of giggles, in style it's grown.
So cherish this gem, it's much more than bling,
An elegance housed in a jester's wing.

www.ingramcontent.com/pod-product-compliance
Lightning Source LLC
Chambersburg PA
CBHW051736290426
43661CB00123B/472